Original title:
Birch Bark Ballads

Copyright © 2025 Creative Arts Management OÜ
All rights reserved.

Author: Liam Sterling
ISBN HARDBACK: 978-1-80567-175-6
ISBN PAPERBACK: 978-1-80567-474-0

Echoes of the Woodland Echo

In the woods, a squirrel plays,
Chasing shadows, in a daze.
A raccoon trudges with great flair,
Wearing boots, thinking he's rare.

The owl hoots a silly song,
Laughing at the things gone wrong.
A rabbit hops with comic grace,
And trips upon a mushroom space.

Whispers of the Woodland Veil

Under leaves so green and bright,
Frogs hold concerts late at night.
A bear hums a playful tune,
Dancing 'neath the silver moon.

The deer prance in a funny line,
Trying hard to look divine.
Yet they stumble, what a sight,
As the owls cheer with delight.

Beneath the Shimmering Bark

A chipmunk juggles acorns round,
Falling down without a sound.
The trees giggle as they sway,
Whispering secrets of the day.

A fox in shades, he struts about,
Claiming he knows what it's about.
But he slips and lands in a stream,
And the fish laugh at his big dream.

The Pulse of the Timbered Heart

The wind carries tales so wild,
Of a lost and wayward child.
Who thought he'd find a treasure there,
But discovered frogs, a lively pair.

The brook bubbles with a laugh,
As squirrels make a silly craft.
They gather twigs and leaves galore,
Building nests that float and soar.

The Calm within the Canopy

In the tree's embrace we sit,
Holding laughter, not a bit.
Squirrels scurry, jokes take flight,
Under branches, all feels right.

Birds engage in loud debate,
Who can fly the highest rate?
Leaves rustle, secrets share,
Nature's giggle fills the air.

A Forest's Heartbeat

In the woods, the trees conspire,
To tease the sun, they raise the fire.
A bear grins with a berry stash,
While rabbits hop, a comical clash.

Acorns fall like tiny bombs,
Wildly rolling, nature's charms.
The forest hums a silly tune,
As shadows dance beneath the moon.

Strong and True

Mighty oaks and wobbly pines,
Compete in strength through twisty lines.
One decides to strike a pose,
But trips and tumbles—oh, how it goes!

A chipmunk mocks with tiny glee,
"Look at that dance, it's just for me!"
Roots entwined in playful fights,
Nature's humor under the lights.

The Harmonious Embrace of Shadows

In shadow play, the trees all tease,
Swaying softly in the breeze.
Frogs croak jokes beneath the glow,
While crickets chirp a nightly show.

Mice wear hats made out of leaves,
Giggling softly, oh how it weaves!
Underfoot, the mushrooms laugh,
At squirrels' antics on their path.

Reveries from Deep Within the Wood

Dreamers nestle, snug and warm,
In the forest's funny charm.
A woodpecker, with rhythm right,
Beats the drum, a goofy sight.

The mossy couch is where we lie,
Giggling as the clouds float by.
Whimsy dances in the glade,
As critters join the masquerade.

Legends of the Whispering Green

In a forest where critters spark,
Squirrels nibble on a tree's remark.
Frogs croon tunes, a joyous cheer,
While the owls hoot, 'You're late, my dear!'

A raccoon wearing a tiny hat,
Struts by, looking rather fat.
He steals the corn, a playful theft,
And leaves without a tiny left.

The foxes dance in moonlit rays,
Chasing shadows in funny ways.
While bunnies laugh at their own dash,
Their thumping feet create a splash.

So gather 'round the giggling stream,
Where laughter curls and joys redeem.
In whispering green, joy takes flight,
Turning each day into pure delight.

Dance of the Quaking Leaves

Leaves that shiver in a breeze,
Rustle gently, if you please.
A squirrel spins a grand ballet,
As sunlight teases, bright and gay.

Dancing to a rhythm sweet,
The branches sway with lively beat.
A porcupine shows off his moves,
While all the woodland laughs and grooves.

Rabbits twirl in a playful race,
Chasing shadows, what a place!
Chipmunks cheer, "You'll win for sure!"
While the wise owl grins, 'I'm secure.'

The forest hums with giggles bright,
Underneath the soft moonlight.
In this dance, there's no demand,
Just funny steps, nature's band.

Symphony of Starlit Silhouettes

Under stars, shadows boldly play,
Silhouettes laugh in their own way.
A hedgehog sings in off-key pitch,
While ants march by, they have no glitch.

Owls join in with a hoot-hoot song,
Singing softly, right or wrong.
Beneath the moon, it's quite a sight,
Even the trees sway with delight.

A raccoon drums on a hollow log,
While crickets chirp; they're quite the slog.
Fireflies twinkle in sync, what fun,
Lighting up the night like none!

This symphony in the cool night air,
Brings laughter, joy, beyond compare.
In starlit shadows, life's so grand,
With funny tales from critter band.

Woven Words in Wistful Woods

In wistful woods where whispers loom,
Stories dance from twig to bloom.
A spider spins her tangled tale,
Of brave little ants who never fail.

A wolf howls softly, seeking friends,
It's funny how the laughter blends.
Deer prance by with stylish grace,
While frogs croak, trying to keep pace.

Thoughts are woven in golden glow,
As chipmunks argue over the show.
A bear rearranges the show's score,
Saying, "You missed, come back for more!"

With every word and every cheer,
The forest echoes tales we hear.
In wistful woods, camaraderie shines,
Crafting laughter inside the pines.

Nature's Ballads in the Breeze

A squirrel danced on a branch,
His acorns did he prance.
With nuts he took a chance,
He spun in a silly stance.

Birds chirped jokes with delight,
While flowers bloomed in bright.
The grass tickled a kite,
As it soared to a great height.

A frog croaked a funny tale,
Of a dog who chased his tail.
With hops that made him flail,
Their laughter set the trail.

In nature's comedic cheer,
Every creature is sincere.
They share a joke or jeer,
As the world spins, oh so clear.

A Treetop Tale in Moonlight

Under the glow of the moon,
A raccoon sang a tune.
He danced with a cartoon,
While fireflies joined in soon.

The owls hooted in jest,
Claiming they knew the best.
A joke that put to test,
Whose wings would win the quest.

A sloth hung upside down,
While the sky wore a frown.
He said, "I'll take the crown,
But first, I'll take a nap now!"

With laughter in the night,
Nature spun her delight.
In sky's soft twilight,
Jokes fluttered, taking flight.

Timeless Stories on Nature's Stage

In the heart of the woods,
Where everyone understood,
A bear wore leafy hoods,
And pranced as best he could.

A rabbit spun a tale,
Of a snail that dared to sail.
His stories would prevail,
Aging slow like old ale.

The deer giggled so bright,
At a fox in awkward flight.
In shadows, they'd ignite,
The sweetest of laughter's light.

Thus nature tells her jest,
In whispers, they are blessed.
With every creature's quest,
The stage of life is dressed.

The Murmurs of Quiet Groves

In quiet groves, a crow spoke,
Telling tales of a lost cloak.
With each whimsical yoke,
Giggling under the oak.

A chipmunk wore a tiny hat,
While the badger chased a cat.
They paused for a chitchat,
As mischief sat on the mat.

The dusky light played its hand,
As shadows danced on the sand.
All joined the merry band,
In a laughter-filled land.

From whispers amongst the leaves,
To the buzzing of the bees,
Nature weaves and retrieves,
The joy that never leaves.

Shadows Beneath the Great Canopy

Under branches thick and wide,
Squirrels chatter, none can hide.
The raccoons plot in low tones,
While owls laugh in silly groans.

Leaves do dance on breezy highs,
As chipmunks trade their silly lies.
A crow caws jokes no one gets,
In nature's court, there are no debts.

The sun peeks through, a golden spy,
Spreading laughter from the sky.
Nature's jesters take their stage,
With antics fit for any age.

From the roots to branches tall,
Nature whispers, "Join the call!"
So let us skip in light and play,
In the woods, it's a funny day.

Frosted Leaves and Twilight Tales

When the frost begins to creep,
The forest giggles, wakes from sleep.
A fox dons a snowy cap,
With dreams of mischief — what a trap!

Twilight paints the sky in hues,
Where shadows dance in quirky shoes.
Even the owls can't help but wink,
As twilight tales unfold by the creek.

The trees wear coats of frosted lace,
Chasing off the squirrel race.
While crickets sing 'neath silver gleam,
Sparking joy in every dream.

Nature chuckles, shares her lore,
In winter's chill, there's always more.
So gather close, hear stories sway,
In frost and leaves, we laugh and play.

The Rustling Voice of Nature

In the rustling leaves, a secret stirs,
As wanderers giggle, teasing furs.
A badger rolls in leaf confetti,
While butterflies flaunt, looking jetty.

The wind tells tales with twirling glee,
Of ants who dance on bended knee.
A rabbit trips, then strikes a pose,
While nature laughs, nobody knows.

Crickets chirp their witty song,
As trees sway lightly, all day long.
The brook bubbles with hearty cheer,
A bubbling voice for all to hear.

Under the sun, that laughing sway,
We join the nature's funny play.
In rustling whispers, joy abounds,
In every heartbeat, laughter sounds.

Bark and Breath of Ancient Times

In the forest where stories bloom,
Old trees whisper from their gloom.
With bark like skin, they laugh and tease,
Echoing tales carried in the breeze.

Ancient roots hold giggles deep,
As history plays with a joyful leap.
Fungi with hats join the parade,
In this land where laughter's made.

A woodpecker's tap is a quirky beat,
As woodland critters find their seat.
Time-travelers in their playful jive,
Amongst the wooden giants, we thrive.

With breath of ages mingling still,
Nature's joy could never chill.
So join the dance, and let's embrace,
The ancient mirth in this sacred place.

A Dance of Natural Elegance

In the forest where critters sway,
Branches laugh and start to play.
Squirrels wear their dapper hats,
While raccoons dance with sassy chats.

Fluttering leaves join in the fun,
A ticklish breeze, oh what a run!
Trees twirl with a mighty cheer,
Nature's ball, with no one near.

Bumblebees buzz a little tune,
Chasing shadows 'neath the moon.
Mice in slippers take the floor,
While crickets chirp for an encore.

Joyful whispers, soft and light,
In the woods, everything feels right.
With nature's laugh, we can't resist,
A dance of fun, too good to miss.

The Trunks that Hear All

Old trunks stand with ears so wide,
Listening to secrets, they confide.
Squirrels gossip, with twitching tails,
While owls hoot their midnight tales.

Mice plot schemes beneath the bark,
While raccoons laugh until it's dark.
The trees chuckle at the chatter,
Leaves quiver with each whispered matter.

Foxes stretch, then roll in leaf,
Creating chaos, oh, what a thief!
Nature's gossip, all around,
In the woodland, laughter's found.

If trunks could speak, what tales they'd tell,
Of antics wild, they'd do so well.
A concert of giggles fills the air,
In the heart of the woods, the joy we share.

Melodies of the Forest Floor

Underfoot, the forest sings,
Leaves and roots wear silly rings.
Frogs croak out their sporty beat,
While bugs tap dance with tiny feet.

Ants march on in perfect lines,
While mushrooms giggle, making signs.
A shuffle here, a hop and sway,
Nature's tune comes out to play.

The sun spills gold on mossy beds,
Where rabbits nap and scratch their heads.
Everyone joins in with glee,
Writing songs of harmony.

At dusk, the critters start to roam,
Chasing shadows, calling home.
The forest floor, a joyful place,
Where every creature finds its grace.

Patterns of Dreams in Leafy Shadows

In the shade where sunlight gleams,
Leafy patterns weave like dreams.
Raccoon scribbles art with paws,
While squirrel giggles, gives a pause.

Breezes carry whispers soft,
Grass blades dance and twirl aloft.
The shadows play their hands ajar,
Singing songs where wonders are.

Winks from critters, drinks from dew,
Delight hides in every hue.
The trees sway, a merry crew,
Creating laughter, pure and true.

In leafy shadows, hearts take flight,
As every moment feels so right.
A tapestry of dreams entwined,
Nature's humor, intertwined.

A Tapestry of Tender Growth

Little squirrels dance on high,
Chasing leaves that flutter by.
Underneath a dancing sun,
Who knew nature could be fun?

Jumpy rabbits race a hare,
Wobbling legs, quite a rare flair.
In the grass, the ants complain,
"Why's it always us in vain?"

Birds are giggling in the trees,
Singing songs that tease the bees.
Frogs croak out a leaping tune,
Making friends with the round moon.

Raccoons peek with playful glee,
Plotting mischief from a tree.
In this wild and vibrant show,
Nature's humor steals the glow!

Nature's Melodic Canvas

A raccoon with a fancy hat,
Danced atop a cozy mat.
He yelled, "Look at my smooth moves!"
While following the funky grooves.

Bumblebees in a tango spin,
Marked their rhythm with a grin.
Flowers laughed, swaying slow,
To the buzz that stole the show.

A cheeky crow let out a caw,
As if he'd teach us full of awe.
But tripped on branches in mid-flight,
Turning day into pure delight.

The brook babbled, full of cheer,
Whispering, "Come and sit right here!"
Nature's symphony, a great burst,
In playful tones so well rehearsed!

Tales from the Silent Grove

In the grove where whispers play,
A fox tells tales of his ballet.
Otters giggle, rolling round,
As mischief in their hearts is found.

A stoic owl gives quite the stare,
Yet can't hide his feathered flair.
Squirrels leap, making a bet,
On who'll steal the last sunset.

The trees lean in, quite intrigued,
As critters' antics are perceived.
The pine trees chuckle, "Oh my dear,
It's a show we can't help but cheer!"

Underneath the silver moon,
Nature's laughter is a tune.
In this grove, no hush or frown,
Just a party without a crown!

The Hollow Music of Timber

A tree trunk speaks with a low voice,
"Why did the twig make that choice?"
Bouncing berries start to joke,
As mushrooms join in, quite bespoke.

Woodpeckers tap their native beat,
While the groundhogs wiggle their feet.
Wandering winds add to the fun,
With notes that only trees have spun.

In the silence of the bark,
Chirping crickets light a spark.
Each branch sways with a silly dance,
Inviting all to join the chance.

With laughter echoing through the wood,
Every critter plays as they should.
Nature sings in vibrant tones,
Turning timber into the funniest puns!

The Dance of Nature's Skin

The trees wear coats of white and brown,
They sway and giggle, twirl around.
Leaves rustle secrets, loud and clear,
Nature laughs, come join the cheer.

A squirrel hops with style and grace,
Wearing acorns like a silly face.
Branches join in, a clapping delight,
Jumpy critters dance through the night.

Mossy carpets and shoelace vines,
Nature's breath makes funky signs.
Under the moon, all creatures sing,
Forget your worries, let joy take wing.

Nature's skin is a playful sight,
With every breeze, a comical flight.
So gather round, let laughter soar,
In the forest, there's always more.

Barksong of the Forest

In the woods, a melody plays,
Barks in harmony, in funny ways.
The pines hum softly, a tune so sweet,
While oaks stomp rhythm with big, flat feet.

A raccoon shimmies, all dressed in fur,
As songbirds chirp, they start to purr.
Funky fungi tap dance around,
With laughter echoing all around.

Nature's choir, a jolly crew,
With whispers of leaves, making do.
Logs drumming beats, a wild parade,
All critters join, not one afraid.

A chorus of giggles, a canopy show,
In woodland wonders, laughter will flow.
Barksong ringing, sweet as a wink,
Join in the fun, and don't you think!

Memories of the Ancient Trunks

Ancient trunks, with tales to tell,
Whispering stories, casting a spell.
Sprightly saplings curve their backs,
While tree folks wink from leafy stacks.

With each knot and ring of age,
A hidden tale, a page by page.
They chuckle softly with the winds,
In memories where the laughter spins.

Branches stretch like arms in play,
Dancing gently, come what may.
Old roots grip tight, in games of chance,
Allowing nature a silly glance.

The wisdom of ages wrapped in bark,
Hidden humor in each little mark.
Come join the laughter, come take a look,
In the stories written in each old nook.

The Language of Leaves and Dreams

Leaves chatter softly, secrets they share,
In wind-blown whispers fluttering there.
A dreamer's mind, a playful flight,
As drowsy afternoons turn into night.

Frolicking shadows on the ground,
In nature's jest, lost dreams abound.
A chipmunk giggles, with mischief alive,
In a world where bumbles and chuckles thrive.

Sunlight dapples, like laughter bright,
Creating giggles in joyful light.
The breeze brings puns through trees and sky,
As leaves tumble down, with a playful sigh.

Nature's language, a joyous hum,
With every rustle, more laughter to come.
Come join the tossing, and take a dive,
In dreams woven where the giggles thrive.

The Unfolding of Eternal Rings

In the woods, a tree did sigh,
Leaves like laughter floated high.
Rings of age, a wise old jest,
Counting years, it thinks it's best.

Squirrels dance and leap with glee,
Chasing shadows, just like me.
Branches wave, a playful show,
Winking at the world below.

Roots do tickle, twigs do tease,
Nature's jokes blow in the breeze.
Carved with humor, each small groove,
In this forest, we all move.

So grab a laugh, a twig or two,
Join the fun, there's room for you.
With every chuckle, trees will sway,
In the woods, let's laugh today!

Melodies Born from the Forest's Breath

In the rustling leaves, a tune,
Bees hum softly to the moon.
Birds in chorus chirp and chirp,
While ants march by in quite the burp!

Mice hold concerts, cheese in hand,
Twirling disco, oh so grand.
Tree stumps serve as dance floors vast,
Nature's party, none can outlast.

With every drip from leaves above,
A rhythm crafted, full of love.
Logs entreat with beats so round,
A symphony where joy is found.

So join the fun, a woodland spree,
Nature's laughter sets us free.
Let the tunes of forest sing,
In this place, just let it swing!

The Poetry of Timbered Silhouettes

Standing tall, the trees all giggle,
Casting shadows, they do wiggle.
Branches bend, a playful bow,
Whispering tales, 'Look at me now!'

Woodpeckers drum like joyful bands,
While chipmunks draw in tree-side sands.
With every sway, a spirit wakes,
Dancing to laughter, the forest quakes.

Leaves flutter down, a gentle cheer,
Rustling secrets, coming near.
One big trunk, a joker's play,
Spreads its arms, inviting sway.

So let's carve smiles in the bark,
As sun sets low, we'll stroll in dark.
In this timbered world, found a seat,
Nature's laugh makes life so sweet!

Nature's Story in a Wandering Breeze

Whispers float on a gentle breeze,
Telling tales among the trees.
Leaves gossip in a funny tone,
As squirrels roll their acorn throne.

Clouds drift by with a giggly grin,
As flowers bloom, let the fun begin!
Bees in tuxes, buzzing proud,
Dancing on petals, quite the crowd.

A wayward twig trips a tiny hare,
Jumping high, but without a care.
Nature chuckles, sharing the jest,
A story told, we laugh at best.

So listen close to the wind's soft song,
It tells of fun where we belong.
In this playful world, let's unwind,
Nature's laughter is one of a kind!

The Symphonies of Ages Past

In the forest, sounds collide,
Squirrels chatter, nothing to hide.
Acorn drums beat the sky,
Trees do a dance, oh my!

Frogs croak tunes from the creek,
Mice intone, not so meek.
The wind hums a silly song,
Nature's chorus, never wrong!

Leaves twirl in a jovial spree,
Branches wiggle with glee.
Mushrooms sway, one foot in,
A merry jig in their skin!

Oh, what a ruckus, quite absurd,
Even the fox joins, undeterred.
In this symphony of delight,
We'll party through the night!

Whispers of Woodland Journeys

In the woods, a tale unfolds,
With whispers that giggle and scold.
The path winks, sly in the shade,
What silly trouble have we made?

A raccoon plays peek-a-boo,
While owls plot their next to-do.
Each step crackles, a cheeky tease,
As if the forest aims to please!

The pine trees giggle, swaying tall,
As squirrels plan a nutty ball.
"Who knew the woods could be so grand?"
As every traveler takes a stand.

We skip through shadows, laughter bright,
In woodland journeys, sheer delight.
May every twist bring a grin,
For mischief thrives where we begin!

Inked by Nature's Breath

With colors from the sunlit sky,
Nature paints with a cheeky sigh.
Daisies giggle in vibrant hues,
While breezes share the latest news.

Bumblebees buzz with grand intent,
Spreading laughter wherever they went.
Each petal's a note in this song,
Nature's canvas, bright and strong.

The grass plays patty-cake on the ground,
While the trees sway without a sound.
Ink of laughter fills the air,
In a whimsical world without a care!

Join the dance, let joy express,
A tapestry of fun, no less!
Inked by whispers, all around,
In nature's heart, we are found!

Echoes of Roots and Branches

Roots grumble in their tangled beds,
While branches gossip overhead.
What secrets do the old trees keep?
As the forest stirs from its sleep.

The shadows chuckle, side by side,
As playful breezes take a ride.
A fox struts, tail held up high,
Waving to clouds that dance in the sky.

In the underbrush, laughter issues,
Echoing softly between the tissues.
Moss mutters jokes, not too witty,
While puddles reflect the city!

So join the roots and branches wide,
In this jesting spree, we abide.
For in the woods, the spirit thrives,
Where the echoing joy of nature strives!

The Soul of the Whispering Foliage

In the woods where squirrels prance,
Leaves gossip while breezes dance.
Whispers tickle the old oak tree,
   As branches laugh in unity.

Mice debate what cheese to steal,
While rabbits plot their next big meal.
The shadows stretch and chatter too,
   As sunlight joins the fun anew.

Harmonies in the Hush of Green

Crickets sing their twilight song,
In the creek, the frogs sing along.
A turtle slips with a silly grin,
As caterpillars spin their spin.

Owls hoot with a wise old tone,
As fireflies flash, they're never alone.
Nature's concert fills the night,
With every laugh, pure delight.

Nature's Heartbeat and Whispers of Air

The wind giggles through the grass,
As dandelions shake their sass.
A breeze nudges a passing bee,
Who's busy plotting a honey spree.

Clouds are sheep, fluffy and bright,
Drifting lazily, what a sight!
Nature chuckles under the sun,
In this world, we all have fun.

Wooded Secrets and Open Skies

A raccoon with a mask so sly,
Steals snacks without a hint of shy.
While woodpeckers knock on tree trunks,
Nature's way of sharing some junk.

The river flows like a tongue-in-cheek,
Telling jokes as it starts to speak.
Under the moon, the shadows play,
In wooden realms where we laugh all day.

Echoing Lullabies of the Pines

In the forest, trees do sway,
Whispering secrets of the day.
Squirrels chatter, quite the show,
While chipmunks dance below the snow.

Frogs are croaking loud and clear,
Their chorus brings a giggling cheer.
Bunnies bounce with silly glee,
Waving to the ladybug, you see?

Clouds drift by with perfect style,
A windy gust makes branches smile.
Nature's jesters, all around,
Spin their tales without a sound.

So, lie back on the forest floor,
Let laughter echo, evermore.
In this vast, green, playful land,
Life's absurdity is well-planned.

Nature's Fragile Pages

Leaves like pages, turn with ease,
Stories written by the breeze.
Bees are scribbling in the air,
Joking 'bout the flowers' flair.

The playful brook runs fast and free,
Splashing tales of whimsy, see?
Pebbles giggle, jumping high,
While dragonflies flirt and fly.

Mice are plotting with a grin,
Their tiny tails, a whirl within.
Mushrooms pop up, quite the crew,
Waiting for a fancy dew.

Nature's humor, mild yet bold,
Tales unfold, so sweetly told.
In this realm of funny sights,
Every creature sparks delights.

Reverie in the Rustic Realm

In the meadow, sheep converse,
Each one dreaming, quite diverse.
Grasshoppers play a fiddle tune,
As the sun sets, nodding 'oon.

Wandering winds tell silly jokes,
Bringing laughter to the folks.
Daisies dance, so bright and white,
Cheering up the starry night.

Owls wear glasses, wise and grand,
Reading jokes from nature's hand.
Raccoons giggle, stealing pies,
Crafty plans in moonlit skies.

So linger long beneath the trees,
With nature's laughter in the breeze.
In every rustle, hint a jest,
A simple playground, we're so blessed.

The Charms of Canopy Stories

Up above, the treetops chat,
Sharing tales of where they're at.
Parrots squawk a punchline sweet,
While monkeys join with laughter neat.

Twigs are whispering, 'Have some fun!',
Pretending to be old and done.
While owls roll their eyes in glee,
At all the antics they can see.

Sunlight dances through the leaves,
Painting shadows, making peeks.
Squirrels toss acorns in their games,
Calling out each other's names.

So listen close to nature's glee,
Where every nook holds mystery.
The charm of life, in every cheer,
Etches smiles, bringing us near.

The Gentle Call of Timber Trails

In the woods, the squirrels play,
Dancing on branches, come what may.
Raccoons wear masks, oh what a sight,
Stealing snacks under the moonlight.

Birds gossip loud, perched high in a tree,
Chirping secrets, wild and free.
A chipmunk runs, his cheeks so round,
With acorns hidden, treasures abound!

A deer stumbles, tripping on twigs,
While frogs leap high, doing little gigs.
The laughter of nature fills the air,
With silly moments, made to share.

Fungi frolic beneath a log,
Toadstools whisper, "Come dance along!"
The gentle call, a fun parade,
In timber trails, let's not be delayed.

The Heartbeat of Nature's Ink

Nature's pen writes tales of glee,
A bear's good dance, oh wow, let's see!
With clumsy paws, he takes the floor,
While birds in chorus, cheer and roar.

A beaver builds with joyful pride,
His dam's a wonder, a water slide!
Oh, how he splashes, what a sight,
Turning logs to pure delight.

Crickets drum with legs so fine,
While fireflies flicker, like stars that shine.
In this ink, the wild does play,
With chuckles echoing every day.

The wind plays tunes through leaves so bright,
Nature's heartbeat, a pure delight.
Every laugh, every quirk, a joyful link,
In the pages of life, where nature's ink.

Echoes of the Emerald Veil

Hidden whispers in leaves so lush,
The gnomes giggle with every brush.
Echoes of laughter, soft and sweet,
As fairies dance on nimble feet.

A fox in a scarf struts with flair,
While hedgehogs roll without a care.
They tumble down the emerald hill,
With joyful squeals, they fit the bill!

Mushrooms giggle in circles tight,
As toads croak tunes beneath the night.
The secrets of the woods unfold,
In melodies of green and gold.

The echoes linger, the fun won't cease,
In this veil, nature finds its peace.
With every chuckle, and every cheer,
Life's a party, let's all draw near!

The Swaying Rhythms of Life

In the breeze, the tall grass bends,
Nature's dance that never ends.
The wiggle of worms, a little jig,
Every move, so bright and big!

The brook babbles tales of cheer,
With rock skipping contests far and near.
Frogs leap high, the winner's king,
Crowned with lily pads, a funny thing!

Bumblebees buzz with busy gait,
In this rhythm, they never wait.
While butterflies flaunt, oh so bold,
In colors bright, their stories told.

The swaying trees, they join the fun,
Their branches sway in the setting sun.
In these rhythms, life's sweet songs,
Where laughter lives and joy belongs.

Rhythm of the Rustic Wilderness

A squirrel did dance on a tree limb high,
While a crow cawed laughter from the nearby sky.
The raccoon wore a hat that was way too small,
And told goofy tales that made the woodpeckers haul.

The frogs held a concert in the muddy creek,
Their croaks like a chorus, quirky and meek.
The chipmunks gathered for some acorn stew,
Chasing their tails, while the owls hooted too.

A bear in a tutu twirled with delight,
Spinning 'round firs like it's party night.
With each silly stumble, the forest would cheer,
For nature's own comedy year after year.

So come join the rhythm where laughter's the song,
In this playful haven where none can go wrong.
With critters all giggling under leaves so green,
Nature's own antics are a sight to be seen.

Leaves Speak in Soft Murmurs

The leaves had a secret, they whispered in glee,
Of a mischievous fox who drank too much tea.
He stumbled on roots, said, "What a wild dream!"
As the trees chuckled softly, a verdant team.

The bumblebees buzzed with a comedic sting,
While the flowers all swayed, pretending to sing.
A butterfly pirouetted in splendid array,
And the grasshoppers laughed, shouting, "Dance all day!"

Old moss on the rocks said with a funny croak,
"I once was a tree but turned into a joke!"
A snail pondered life from its shell—what a view,
While the sun overhead beamed a golden hue.

Thus the leaves keep on murmuring tales of delight,
Of critters and stories in day and in night.
Nature's own jesters weave laughter like thread,
In the great leafy theater where humor is bred.

Labyrinth of Timbered Thoughts

In a maze made of wood where squirrels conspire,
One whispered to trees, sparked heart's old fire.
"Why did the owl cross the logging road?"
To earn its big wings and lighten the load!"

The pine trees chuckled, their needles all shook,
As raccoons in suits plotted grander hooks.
They dreamed up a scheme for a wild masquerade,
With twigs for their hats, in the glade they paraded.

A hedgehog took stage, with a dance so bizarre,
"This is my moment! I'll shine like a star!"
And the earthworms below sang without any shame,
Belting out tunes with a wiggle and game.

Thus in the timbered paths, tales unfold,
Of laughter and joy, like pockets of gold.
With creatures so quirky, the forest agrees,
Life's a big riddle, unwrapped by the trees.

Shadows on the Forest Floor

Shadows were dancing on the forest floor,
With foxes in top hats, who could ask for more?
A raccoon with a monocle read from the charts,
Reporting on acorns and funny animal arts.

The rabbits were chuckling, baking carrot pie,
While the turtles raced slow, just watching the sky.
A dandelion mocked, blowing seeds in the air,
Saying, "Who needs speed when you've style and flair?"

Sunbeams played hide and seek, oh what fun,
As shadows embraced every leap and every run.
An elk with a top coat claimed, "I'm the king!"
As the creatures all cheered, "What joy do you bring!"

In this playful sanctuary, laughter will soar,
Where shadows weave stories and spirits explore.
For in the woods where the wild things convene,
Every corner of life holds a joke to be seen.

Whispers of the Silver Trees

In the forest, trees do giggle,
Swaying lightly in their wiggle.
Squirrels dance on branches high,
Singing tunes that make birds cry.

Leaves confide in breezes swift,
Sharing secrets, nature's gift.
Rabbits hop with tiny grins,
While the fox just rolls and spins.

Mice hold parties near the creek,
Chasing shadows, hide and seek.
Owls hoot jokes from night's embrace,
As fireflies light up the space.

Laughter echoes, soft, yet bold,
Stories told of days of old.
In this woods, a merry crew,
Come join us, there's room for you!

Echoes from the Woodland Canvas

The trees wear hats of green and brown,
Strutting proudly, never frown.
Bunnies bake with acorn zest,
While bears take afternoon rest.

A raccoon schemes a midnight snack,
Underneath the great oak's back.
With giggles hidden in their paws,
They tease the deer with funny flaws.

The brook sings tunes to jump and dive,
Fish flash by, they're quite alive!
Frogs play ukes with silly songs,
As the evening hum softly throngs.

Crickets tap their tiny feet,
Creating rhythms, oh so sweet.
Each shade dances, shades collide,
In this canvas, joy will bide.

The Secrets of Bark and Breeze

Old trees whisper tales of jest,
Of woodland folk who love to fest.
Chipmunks wear a tiny crown,
Mischief glitters all around.

Squirrels trade their nuts for cheer,
While raccoons hide behind the deer.
With each rustle, wild and bright,
Nature's laughter takes its flight.

Pinecones tumble, rolling fast,
Falling down with every blast.
Woodpeckers drum a catchy beat,
As the air holds laughter sweet.

The breeze carries whims and jokes,
Tickling leaves like playful pokes.
In this realm of glee and sound,
Joyful secrets abound, profound!

Songs of the Whispering Woods

In the woods where whimsy stirs,
Trees wear dresses made of furs.
Each leaf whispers tales insane,
Of a squirrel who loved to train.

Opossums play their silly games,
While hedgehogs claim the forest names.
Fungi swear to hold a ball,
With dancing snails, we will enthrall.

A clever crow tells puns galore,
While Badger begs for just one more.
Textures swirl in light and dark,
As melodies ignite the spark.

Listen close, the woods will sing,
Of funny things that nature brings.
Join the choir, let's unite,
In laughter, morning till night!

Beneath the Leafy Canopy

Beneath the leafy canopy,
Squirrels chatter, oh so sly,
A raccoon wears a fancy hat,
As he steals snacks - my, oh my!

The moose prances, thinks it's grand,
While a porcupine joins the band,
Singing songs to frolic and play,
In a quirky forest wonderland.

A deer drags its friend, a frog,
Who croaks along to every jog,
Caterpillars dance on the ground,
While bees buzz tunes, creating a fog.

Oh, the trees giggle, roots in a twist,
Branches waving, they can't resist,
Nature's laughter fills the air,
In this silly, leafy tryst.

Songs of the Silver Trunk

Songs of the silver trunk begin,
With a fox who sports a wide grin,
He strums a twig like a guitar,
As rabbits hop and dance within.

The owl hoots a nightly joke,
While whispers travel like some smoke,
A badger sways, thinking it jazz,
And blends right in with wiggles, folk.

A crow steals snacks with crafty flair,
But the chipmunks don't seem to care,
For each time he lands with a crash,
They chuckle loud, a playful scare.

With each note, laughter starts to grow,
The forest hums with a vibrant glow,
In this merry, mischievous place,
Where joy and giggles freely flow.

Secrets of the Whispering Woods

Secrets of the whispering woods,
Where mushrooms wear hats, oh so good,
A hedgehog juggles berries with glee,
While a squirrel charms like he should.

The trees gossip, telling tales,
Of raccoons stealing fish with scales,
While the porcupine disco dances,
As he spins past the meadow trails.

Under the moon, the critters play,
With shadows dancing, leading the way,
While fireflies blink like birthday lights,
On this whimsical, wild ballet.

Oh, the sounds are a bright delight,
With laughter echoing through the night,
In the secrets shared beneath their shade,
Joyful spirits take flight.

The Song of the White Trees

The song of the white trees rings loud,
In the hug of the pine, they feel proud,
With squirrels dressed in tiny suits,
They gather all the forest crowd.

A bear trips over its own large paw,
And bushy-tailed fox lets out a guffaw,
While chipmunks hold a talent show,
Each one's act, a funny law.

The wind whispers stupid, silly puns,
As everyone laughs, gumption runs,
A turtle wins the slowest race,
And the rabbit boasts of his fast guns.

With giggles bouncing off the bark,
From dusk till dawn, the woods spark,
In this merry jamboree,
Laughter dances in the dark.

Ode to the Forest Spirits

In the woods, they dance so light,
With twirls that bring laughter bright.
Swaying branches hear their cheer,
Whispers of joy, we hold them dear.

In a pie made of acorn pie,
They sing to the moon up high.
Bouncing squirrels join the song,
In this forest where we belong.

With giggles spread far and wide,
Little sprites take us for a ride.
Jumping logs and teasing vines,
In their world, mischief shines.

O spirits bold, come out to play,
Turn the night into a day.
For in this sacred, wooded dome,
Every heart is called to roam.

Birches Beneath the Stars

Under stars that blink and twink,
Trees sip sunshine with a wink.
Branches whisper silly tales,
While leaves dance like tiny sails.

The trunks wear grins and bark so bright,
Tickling breezes, sheer delight.
Caterpillars laughing while they munch,
On leaves they love, they have a hunch.

Owls hoot jokes in the night air,
While rabbits hop without a care.
Mice in capes join in the fun,
Underneath the moonlit run.

The forest fairies twist and glide,
Making shadows that dance with pride.
In this glade where giggles grow,
Life's a party—now you know!

Songs Carved in Twilight

Twilight sings a silly tune,
As crickets dance beneath the moon.
Branches hum a jazzy beat,
Roots tap-dance with happy feet.

The fireflies join in with glee,
Shining bright for all to see.
Ghosts of leaves swirl in the air,
Playing tricks without a care.

Fungi giggle on the ground,
While mushrooms sway all around.
And in the shadows, something stirs,
A party hat and silly furs.

Time to laugh, time to sing,
In the twilight, joy will spring.
For with whispers of the night,
All things funny come to light.

The Resilient Reference

In the woods, your laughter's heard,
Even from a sleepy bird.
Trees lean in to catch each joke,
As nature's laughter starts to poke.

A beaver, wise in water lore,
Builds his dam, then wants much more.
He fumbles sticks with grace so odd,
Creating ripples, we applaud.

A raccoon's mask, so sly and fun,
Counts all the stars, one by one.
As shadows play on twinkling dew,
The night breathes in a giggling crew.

So here's to memes of bark and green,
In laughter's arms, we have all been.
For every trail we joyfully tread,
Nature's pulse dances, full of red.

Canopy Chronicles

Up in the trees, a squirrel leaps high,
Chasing a bird who just might fly by.
With nuts in his cheeks, he's a clumsy sight,
Yet he winks at the world, feeling just right.

A raccoon with style wears a mask just so,
Dancing in moonlight with all of his glow.
He plunders the picnic, oh what a steal,
With a twirl and a spin, he makes it a meal.

Beneath them, the ants march, minuscule troops,
Carrying crumbs like they're giant loops.
In their tiny parade, oh what a scene,
While the beetles play drums – they're a rockin' machine!

A chatty old owl, wise beyond years,
Tells tales of the night and instills silly fears.
With a wink and a hoot, he nabs the late crowd,
As laughter erupts from the treetops so loud.

Tales of the Tranquil Grove

In the grove so quiet, the buzz is quite grand,
Where rabbits play poker, they never understand.
A hare shuffles cards while munching a sprout,
And giggles erupt when the bluff's called out.

The fireflies flicker, their lights they parade,
While the frogs keep on singing, a ribbit charade.
With a splash and a jump, one makes quite the flop,
The crowd erupts in laughter, they can't make him stop.

On a mossy old stump, the snails gather round,
To discuss all the gossip of who's lost or found.
In their slow, slimy style, they spill all the tea,
With a glimmer of humor, oh so carefree.

Even the clouds join in, puffing out jest,
As they drift by the trees, they're all just a guest.
With each wisp and swirl, they play hide and seek,
Leaving rainbows behind, all giggles and squeaks.

Underneath the White Tree Veil

Beneath the white tree, the whispers are loud,
Where chipmunks debate, feeling so proud.
One touts his acorns, another claims cheese,
As the wind plays along, tickling their knees.

A badger in boots hosts a dance on the greens,
With hedgehogs in sunglasses, oh what a scene!
They cha-cha and shimmy, in a spunky delight,
As the grass sways and giggles, all through the night.

Fireflies flash like they're part of the band,
While crickets compose with a swift, tiny hand.
The whole woodland joins, with a jolly good cheer,
As laughter erupts from the skies oh-so clear.

Together they sway, under moon's silver light,
A parade full of joy that feels just so right.
In a shimmering dream, they frolic and play,
For tomorrow's mischief is just one night away.

Melody of the Woodland Spirits

In the heart of the woods where the mischief is rife,
A bear strums a banjo, living his life.
He kicks up his heels, the squirrels jump high,
As a chorus of creatures sings 'Oh Me, Oh My!'

The chipmunks all dance with their tails in a twirl,
While the fox joins in with a spin and a whirl.
They start up a riot, a fuzzy parade,
With giggles and wiggles, excitement displayed.

An old turtle hums to the beat of the trees,
While the mice tap their feet, moving with ease.
With mushrooms as seats, they groan and they strain,
At the grand woodland festival, oh, what a gain!

With laughter and joy, they wrap up the night,
As stars peek through leaves, adding soft golden light.
In the melody spun by the winks of the sprites,
The woodland's alive, in the heart of delights.

The Language of the Leaves

In the breeze, whispers gleam,
Leaves gossip their silly dream.
They dance and twirl, poke fun,
Sharing secrets, just for fun.

A squirrel sits, ears all perked,
While every tree's a stand-up jerk.
They laugh at clouds, so full of fluff,
Chasing shadows, oh, this is tough!

Roots wiggle, tickling the ground,
Nature's chatter, silly sound.
Laughter spreads, a leafy cheer,
Join in fun, the trees are here!

So listen close, join in the play,
Nature's mirth, a bright ballet.
Each leaf a joker, full of grace,
In this green world, find your place.

Lullabies in Fragile Bark

Moonlight drapes on soft, smooth trees,
Bark croons low in soothing breeze.
Crickets chirp a sleepy tune,
As fireflies blink, they dance till noon.

Nestled close, the night holds tight,
Snuggled critters dream with delight.
Branches sway, a gentle rock,
Telling tales like a clock's tick-tock.

Whispers float, dreams in the air,
Twirling thoughts without a care.
The woods chuckle at the night,
Lullabies bring sweet delight.

Softly now, embrace the charm,
Nature's cradle, safe and warm.
As stars wink in their hushed hark,
Sleep sweetly under fragile bark.

Legends Carved in Nature's Skin

On roots of oak, a silly tale,
Of crafty foxes who like to fail.
They plot and scheme in moonlit spheres,
Then run headfirst, forgetting fears.

The trees bear witness to all the fun,
As squirrels plot and races run.
With nutty schemes and goofy plans,
They scribble legends with tiny hands.

A beaver builds a high-rise home,
While otters slip and gaily roam.
Nature's poets with paws and snouts,
Spin stories loud, with goofy shouts.

So wander wide, explore the bark,
Each notch a story, a hidden spark.
Let laughter echo through the glen,
In wildwood tales, we'll meet again.

Sway of the Silent Stories

In quiet woods where shadows play,
Trees wave hello in a jolly way.
With every breeze, a chuckle stirs,
Their whispered tales are soft as purrs.

Mice in hats with little feet,
Host a party, what a treat!
Cupcakes made of leaves and dew,
Join us now, there's room for you!

Chirping birds sing funny rhymes,
Filling the air with joyful chimes.
Owl rolls eyes, quite unimpressed,
"Why are we all so overly stressed?"

So listen near, with heart so light,
In this realm, all feels just right.
Nature's laughter, a real delight,
Sway with the trees into the night!

Nature's Scribe Writes with Green

In the forest where whispers roam,
A squirrel scribbles on a leaf dome.
With acorns as ink and twigs for a pen,
He writes of the day, again and again.

The chipmunks giggle at his clumsy art,
As he scrawls a tale of a runaway cart.
The trees lean in, their laughter so sweet,
While the wind gives a whoosh, a rhythmic beat.

Each blundered word causes quite a stir,
A rabbit hops by, wears a judge's fur.
"Oh listen!" they shout, with a twinkle of glee,
"To nature's own scribe, our bard from the tree!"

With every mistake, the humor runs high,
A chorus of chortles, oh my, oh my!
What tales will he spin, when day turns to night?
In nature's embrace, everything feels right.

Stories from Below the Sky

In the meadow where daisies frolic and play,
A frog with a crown croaks tales every day.
With a wink and a splash, he jumps to the stage,
And turns simple ponds into a magical page.

A mouse with quick feet adds in a twist,
Telling jokes that none could resist.
"The owl thinks he's wise, but I've seen him trip,
Over his own wings, oh what a slip!"

Each little creature gathers around,
For laughter and stories where joy can be found.
A turtle complains, "I'm too slow for the race,"
As the crowd roars in cheer, enjoying the grace.

Beneath the bright sky, they sing without care,
Sharing each moment, a tale to declare.
With giggles and grins that stretch wide and grand,
Together they revel; oh, isn't it grand?

Murmurs of the Forest's Heart

In the heart of the woods, where the shadows dance,
A raccoon debates if he should wear pants.
With a glance at his tail, he shakes his head,
"Why cover my style? I'll go pantsless instead!"

The owls chuckle softly, perched up real high,
As below, a dog barks at a butterfly.
"What's the fuss, dear friend, with your boisterous yelps?"

"It's a flying snack!" he says, "I need it for kelps!"

A badger joins in, with a grin ear to ear,
"Don't chase those sweet wings, my wise little dear!"
With giggles a-plenty, they share their delight,
In the forest's embrace, everything feels bright.

From stumps gathered round, they plot, scheme, and cheer,
Creating new legends that all want to hear.
With laughter as echo, the leaves seem to sway,
In nature's own theater, where we laugh away!

Tapestry of the Leafy Realm

In the realm where squirrels prance,
Leaves are capes in a silly dance.
A raccoon dons a hat so grand,
While chasing crumbs across the land.

Frogs hold court in a puddle wide,
Judging flies that try to glide.
With a croak and a spark of glee,
They mock the bugs' clumsy spree.

Trees gossip in a rustling tone,
Swaying lightly, never alone.
They share tales of the storms' embrace,
And dance with leaves in a windy race.

But watch out for the silly moose,
Wearing socks with no excuse.
He tripped on roots, oh what a sight,
Bursting laughter through the night.

Nature's Nostalgic Narratives.

Old owls rave of nights gone past,
While bunnies hop, their shadows cast.
With tales of nuts and stolen pies,
They whisper truths, oh what a prize!

The trees hum low, their voices deep,
Of crickets' songs that never sleep.
Fireflies twinkle in a grand parade,
Chasing tales in the evening shade.

The meadows teem with clumsy ants,
In line for crumbs, they take their chance.
A tumble here, a slip, a fall,
Yet up they rise, they love the brawl!

Nostalgia wraps the little stream,
Where fish plot out their sneaky scheme.
A splash, a gurgle, much to tease,
Nature's fun is sure to please.

Whispers of the Forest

In shadows deep, the whispers grow,
Of critters prancing to and fro.
A raccoon's theft, a playful trick,
While mockingbirds sing a funny flick.

Squirrels chatter, tails held high,
Debating acorns as they fly.
They argue loud, then shake in mirth,
Claiming jests that crown their worth.

The toad gives tips on catching flies,
In a tuxedo made of vines.
Laughter bubbles from every nook,
As beetles strut with a silly look.

And dancing leaves swirl in delight,
As nature's jesters share the night.
In the forest, fun is the decree,
A merry realm, wild and free.

Echoes from Wooden Dreams

The trees hold secrets, tales are spun,
Of birds who boast, they've just begun.
Each forked twig and hollow knoll,
Echoes laughter, heart and soul.

Chipmunks dart with snacks in tow,
While watching wind as it will blow.
They question why the clouds are grey,
Then laugh it off in splendid play.

The logs might creak with tales so grand,
Of weathered tales and time's command.
They chuckle soft, a devilish gleam,
Living life inside a dream.

So if you listen, you might find,
The forest hums with joy entwined.
In echoes sweet from wooden beams,
Are whispers of our shared daydreams.

www.ingramcontent.com/pod-product-compliance
Lightning Source LLC
Chambersburg PA
CBHW071827160426
43209CB00003B/226